HOW DID IT HAPPEN?

Text by
HOYT JOHNSON

Photos by
TOM JOHNSON

> The immensity of geologic time
> cannot be overstated; nowhere on Earth
> is that more evident than in Sedona
> and Oak Creek Canyon.

Upon viewing Sedona and Oak Creek Canyon for the first time, visitors are spellbound by the spectacular beauty and awesome magnitude of this area's incredible landscape, punctuated by massive red-rock formations that have become renowned throughout the world.

This is, indeed, Red Rock Country, a land that features magnificent sights as unique as any natural splendor on Earth. And testifying to the insatiable curiosity of our civilization, the question that echoes throughout the enchanting canyons that give this area its distinct character, is: "How did it happen?"

Although differences of opinion regarding the geologic history of Sedona's famed sedimentary rocks are yet to be resolved, informed experts agree that this landscape has been more than 350 million years in the making. And they say that the record exposed by geological processes dates back to the ancient Mississippian Period.

Positioned at the temperate base of the Mogollon Rim escarpment — which was carved by perennial Oak Creek and other Verde River tributaries — and surrounded by spires, buttes and mesas, the Sedona area offers earth scientists abundant clues revealed by powerful natural forces. Oak Creek Canyon, eroded into the margin of the Colorado Plateau, provides a complementary exhibit of geological information. This information, when coupled with the great magnitude of history's geologic calendar, helps establish an incredible record of changes that are, indeed, often difficult even to imagine. Nonetheless, a widely accepted scenario of geologic events has been documented in papers and books referred to by members of the world's most elite scientific community.

The Sedona area shares in the more encompassing geological story

Earth Angel Spire in Mormon Canyon is typical of the spectacular red-rock formations that document Sedona's geological history.

One of Sedona's most dramatic exposures of the Schnebly Hill Formation is Mitten Ridge, as seen from Steamboat Rock. Schnebly Hill, higher and composed of light-colored Coconino sandstone, is in the background.

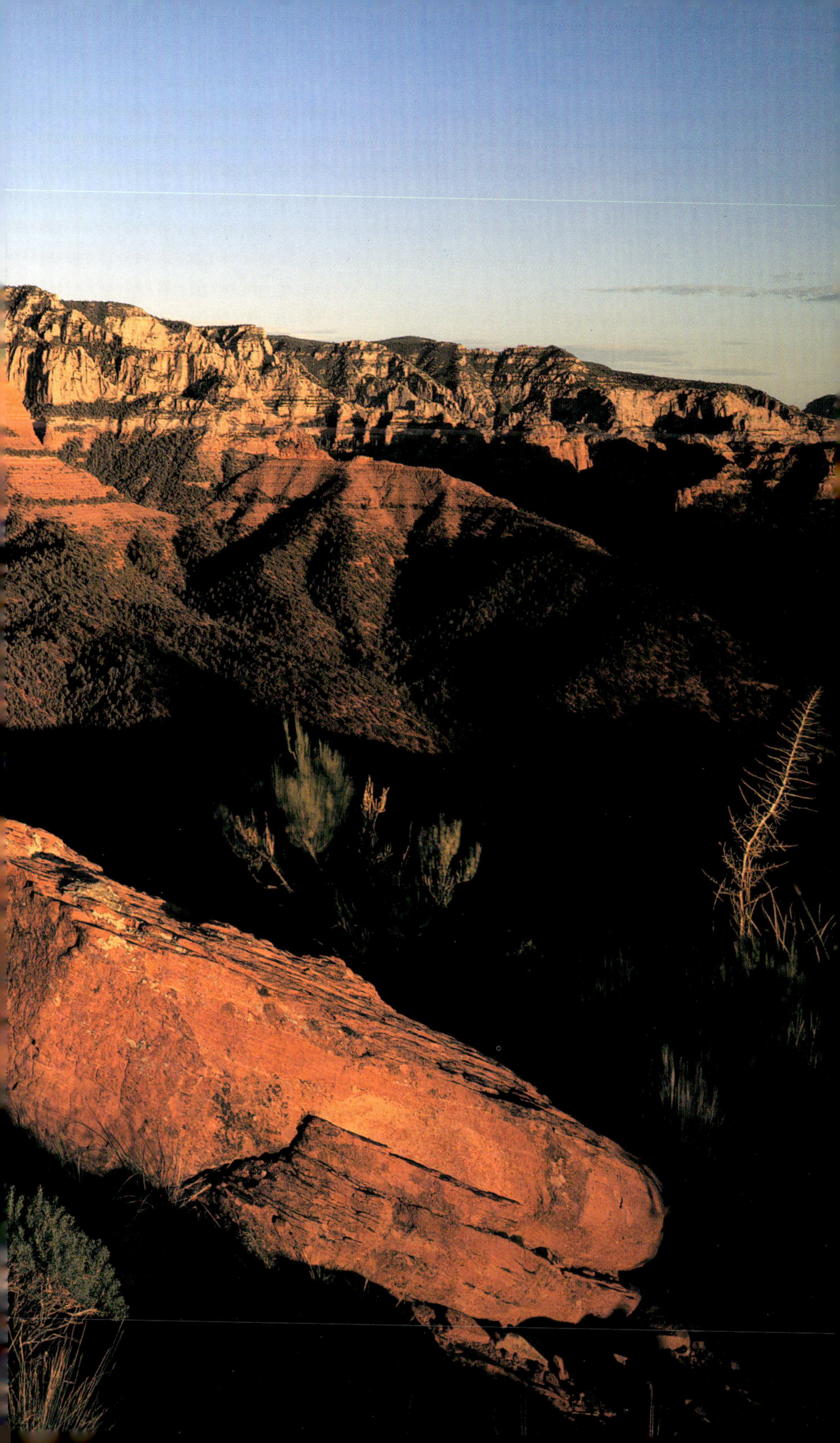

of the southern Colorado Plateau, as well as the central Arizona transition zone. Oak Creek and its canyon are carved into the southern margin of the Colorado Plateau, and Sedona is positioned immediately at the base of this plateau — here, named the Mogollon Rim. This is a high-relief region of canyons, mesas, lesser plateaus and ancient mountain ranges worn down to their ancient roots. Over tremendous spans of time, the area has been blanketed by an accumulation of extremely thick layers of sediment, since turned into rock. The area also has been subjected to uneven uplift, equalization of stresses along fault zones, dissection by erosion and repeated lava flows. To better understand the earth history of this intriguing Red Rock Country, we must first examine the sedimentary rock record. Following this, the mechanisms leading to the development of our modern landscape will be discussed.

In many respects, the sedimentary rocks of Sedona and Oak Creek Canyon are similar to their contemporaries in the classic, upper Grand Canyon region. To those acquainted with the strata of the Grand Canyon, terms such as red-wall limestone, Coconino sandstone and Kaibab Formation will sound familiar when encountered in the Sedona area. The correlation of these strata is simple: they were deposited in large-scale environments such as oceans and coastal deserts. This means that the 80-mile distance between Sedona and the Grand Canyon is nearly inconsequential with regard to types of rocks.

However, problems in correlation occur where strata and rock types defined in one location do not match with seemingly comparable strata and rock types in another area. These discrepancies usually occur in areas where the strata were deposited in relatively small-scale, changing environments — such as a meandering river on a wide flood plain, or a coastal mud flat or bay coupled with fluctuating sea levels. The Supai Group and the Toroweap and Hermit formations are strata that were deposited in changing environments. Therefore, it is difficult to correlate these rock units in the Grand Canyon with those in Sedona.

The oldest strata exposed, and thus the deepest, in the Sedona area are composed of red-wall limestone. These strata are exposed where the Oak Creek Fault crosses Oak Creek between Indian Gardens and Midgley Bridge, and in the bed of Dry Creek, west of Sedona. This red-wall limestone was deposited on a tropical ocean floor during the Early Mississippian Epoch. The rock unit found in the Sedona area is part of a huge limestone bed that can be traced from Mexico into Canada. This limestone was originally an ocean-floor accumulation of shells and corals (whole and crushed), lime mud, remains of single-celled organisms, oolites (lime sand) and chert (siliceous lumps precipitated from sea water).

The Late Mississippian and Early Pennsylvanian epochs are marked by a long cycle of erosion. During this cycle, red-wall limestone formed a bedrock surface — elevated somewhat above sea level — which was etched by streams and scrubbed by wind and

While it is virtually impossible to detail geological history in one sketch, this idealized, stratigraphic "slice" of Oak Creek Canyon and Sedona helps document, in a general way, the chronological "construction" of this unique area.

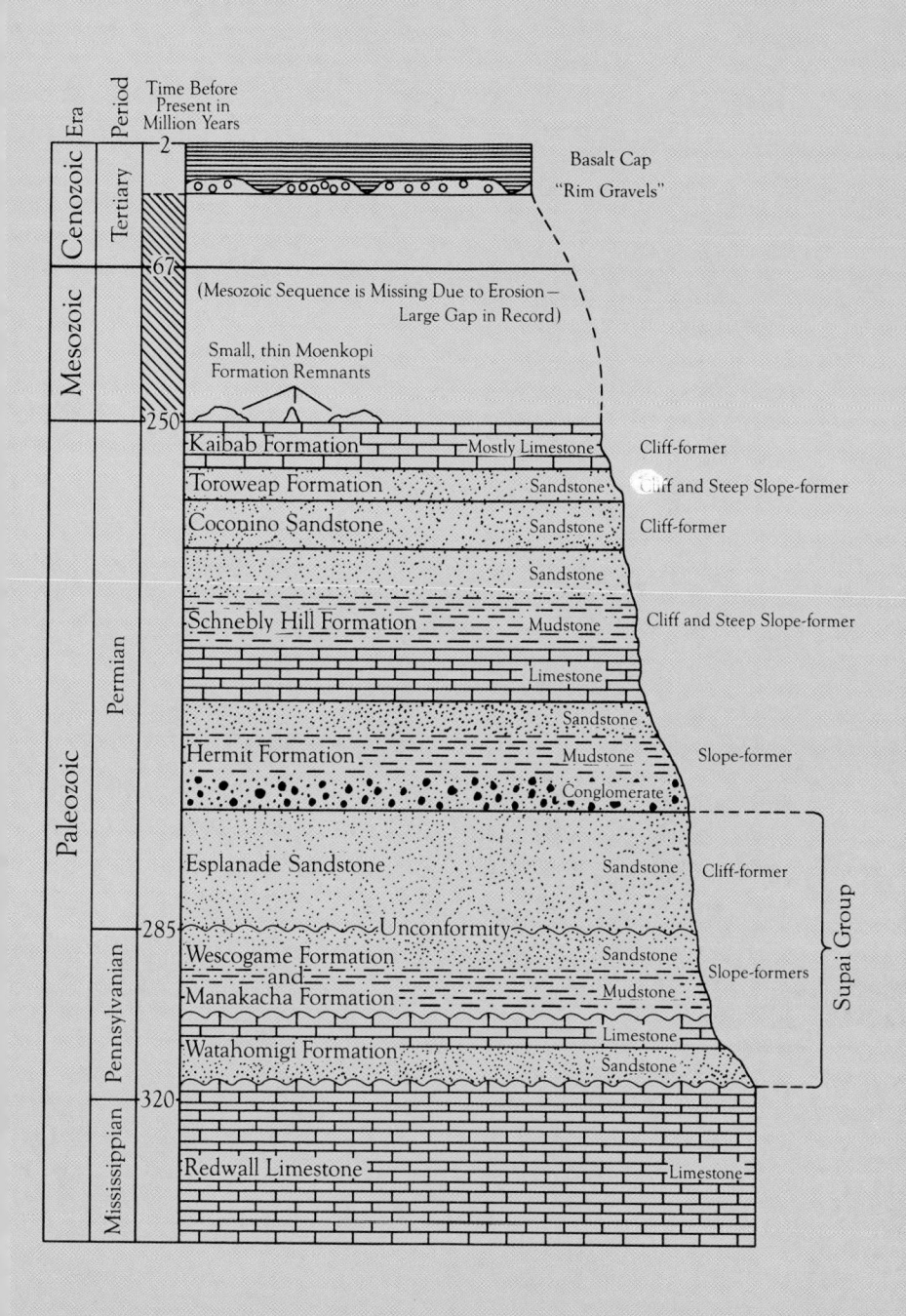

Era	Period	Time Before Present in Million Years	Formation	Rock Type	Feature
Cenozoic	Tertiary	2	Basalt Cap		
			"Rim Gravels"		
Mesozoic		67	(Mesozoic Sequence is Missing Due to Erosion — Large Gap in Record)		
			Small, thin Moenkopi Formation Remnants		
Paleozoic	Permian	250	Kaibab Formation	Mostly Limestone	Cliff-former
			Toroweap Formation	Sandstone	Cliff and Steep Slope-former
			Coconino Sandstone	Sandstone	Cliff-former
				Sandstone	
			Schnebly Hill Formation	Mudstone	Cliff and Steep Slope-former
				Limestone	
				Sandstone	
			Hermit Formation	Mudstone	Slope-former
				Conglomerate	
			Esplanade Sandstone	Sandstone	Cliff-former
	Pennsylvanian	285	Unconformity		
			Wescogame Formation and Manakacha Formation	Sandstone Mudstone	Slope-formers
			Watahomigi Formation	Limestone Sandstone	
	Mississippian	320	Redwall Limestone	Limestone	

Supai Group: Wescogame, Manakacha, Watahomigi, Esplanade Sandstone

It has been determined that the Sedona area was covered by a sea during several geological periods. Today, Ship Rock and Steamboat Rock are anchored in Sedona's unique, red-rock "harbor."

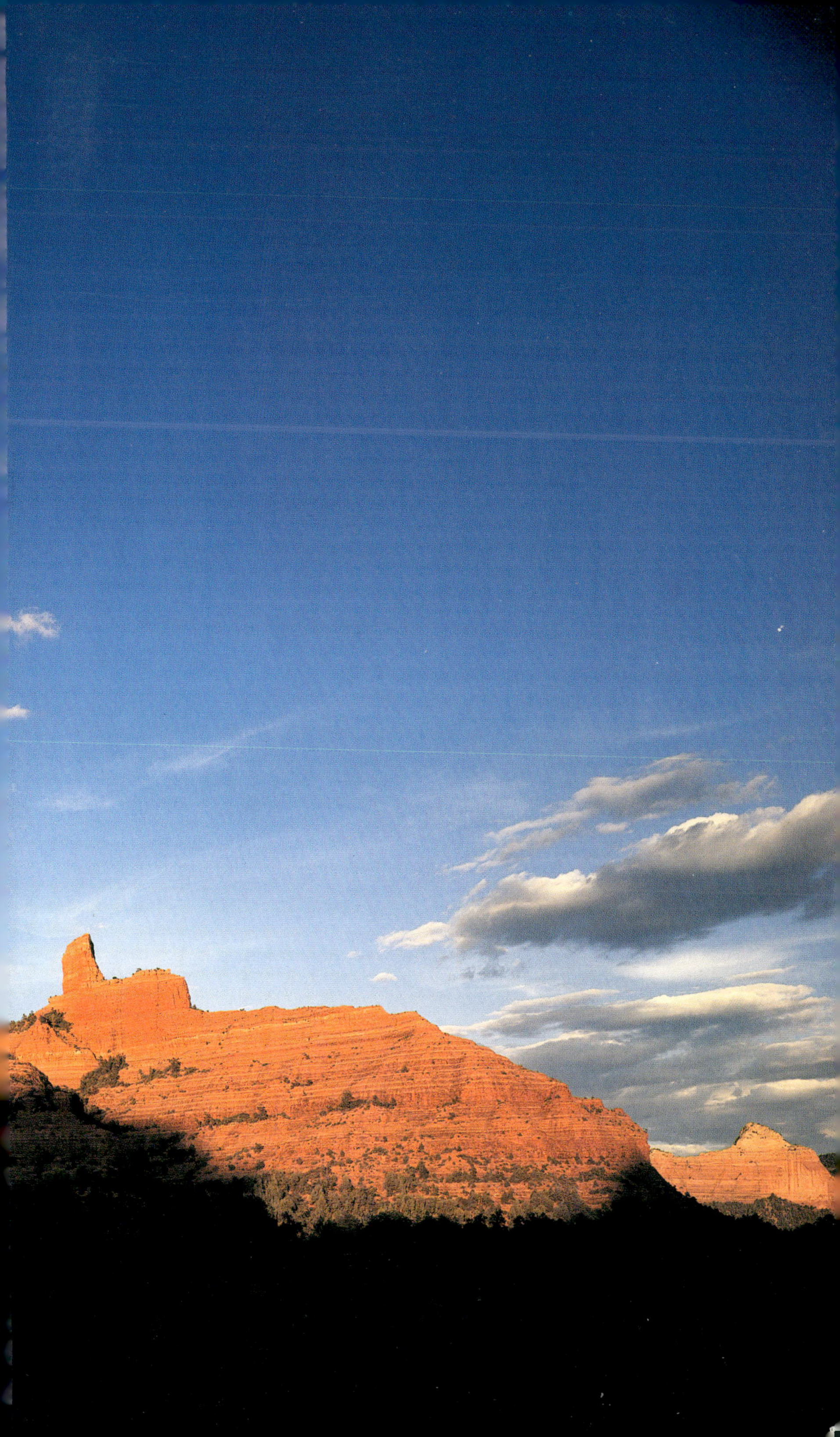

water. Today, this surface shows the marks caused by undulating contact with the next layer of rocks — the Supai Group. The Supai Group is the oldest and lowest in the series of red rocks for which Sedona is famous. These beds of red rocks produced both steep, slick-rock cliffs and more subtle, low-edge, sloped terrain. Exposures of the Supai Group surround Sedona and extend up Oak Creek to form a gorge.

During the Pennsylvanian Period, the Sedona area was close to sea level. The ocean generally remained to the west, though it periodically inundated the region. The Sedona area and Grand Canyon region formed a large embayment of very low elevation into the west coast of North America during this period. The deposition of sediment was cyclical, as were the ocean's transgressions and regressions into and out of the area. Only relatively minor sea-level changes were needed to flood or make a muddy coastal plain of this embayment.

When the shoreline was west of the embayment, sediment that eroded from the highlands to the east and northeast was carried by streams and deposited within the embayment en route to the sea. Evidence suggests that some of the rock contained within the Supai Group was deposited in a mud flat or deltaic environment with meandering sluggish streams. Rock types providing this evidence are mudstones and sandstones that contain plant fossils, crossbedding and channel cuts from shifting streams.

At other times, when the embayment was submerged, large amounts of sediment were deposited — far exceeding the gradual influx of sediment derived from highlands to the east and northeast. Longshore currents moved vast amounts of sand southward along the coast and reworked it into offshore bars, shoals and beaches within the embayment. Today, these deposits are preserved in the Supai Group as red, oxidized sandstone beds containing carbonate grains of fossil material and crossbedded layers much larger than those caused by small streams.

Normal, more-gentle marine conditions also played a role in the development of the Supai Group. Often, we find that thin limestone beds are interspersed between the sandstones and other rocks of the Supai Group. These limestones formed during periods when the sea was able to slowly blanket its floor with its own limey particles, when not overwhelmed by an abundance of land-derived sediment.

Resting upon the Supai Group is the Hermit Formation of the Permian Period. These are the rocks upon which much of the city of Sedona rests. This rock unit only recently has been recognized in the Sedona and Oak Creek Canyon areas. The varied rock types of the Hermit Formation found near Sedona stand in contrast to the homogenous shale that comprises the Hermit Formation of the Grand Canyon. Near Sedona, the Hermit Formation is made up of sandstones, siltstones and conglomerates that indicate it was deposited by meandering streams on a flood plain near sea level. The Hermit Formation is fairly soft and susceptible to erosion; therefore,

Unique red-rock formations dot Fay Canyon, located in the Red Rock-Secret Mountain Wilderness west of Sedona. The secrets of this area are geological, as well as historical.

it weathers to form slopes with low ledges. Often, the Hermit Formation creates the vegetated, rounded "skirts" providing a base for lofty, vertical buttes.

The spectacular red rocks that form the skyline of buttes in southern Oak Creek Canyon and Sedona belong to the recently defined Schnebly Hill Formation. This unit, not present in the Grand Canyon, fills the gap between the Hermit Formation and the well-defined Coconino sandstone. Named for exposures along Schnebly Hill Road, the Schnebly Hill Formation is 900 feet thick and is made up predominantly of sandstone with smaller amounts of mudstone and limestone. Many geologists believe that the Schnebly Hill Formation was laid down in a unique central Arizona basin that derived sediment from the northwest during the Early Permian Epoch. This slowly subsiding basin gathered and preserved sand blown into the area by the prevailing northerly winds of the time. Evidence for the coastal position of the Schnebly Hill Formation is found in a layer of gray Fort Apache limestone. This 6-foot thick, erosion-resistant limestone, found about two-thirds up into the Schnebly Hill Formation, was deposited during a brief period when the basin was inundated by the ocean.

The Schnebly Hill Formation, regarded as the most widely admired rock formation in Red Rock Country, forms the higher parts of many of the buttes in the Sedona area. Among the most dramatic exposures of the Schnebly Hill Formation are Cathedral Rock at Red Rock Crossing and Mitten Ridge east of Midgley Bridge.

Above the Schnebly Hill Formation rests a thick layer of dusty, white Coconino sandstone. This prominent, 500-foot-thick, cliff-forming unit is displayed along the length of Oak Creek Canyon just below the broken limestone and lava on the Mogollon Rim. Perhaps the finest examples of the precipitous Coconino sandstone are exposed in the walls along the West Fork of Oak Creek Canyon, above the red Schnebly Hill Formation.

The wind-deposited, sand-dune origin of the Coconino sandstone is documented by the presence of large-scale crossbedding and by the homogenous, clean sand that composes the rock. These petrified dunes probably originated on an island desert in early Permian times. The sweeping curves of crossbedded planes represent the steep, downwind slopes of dunes that were built up by windward-blown sand. It appears likely that ground water rose up into the dunes, wetting and stabilizing the shifting sand. Waterborne minerals eventually precipitated between the grains of sand, acting as a cement. Trackways of reptiles — lizardlike animals and other wide-bodied, short-legged forms — frequently are found on the faces of these preserved dunes.

The Toroweap Formation in the Grand Canyon is a sandy, silty limestone laid down beneath a shallow sea in early Permian times. In Oak Creek Canyon, however, the Toroweap Formation is predominantly sandstone. This makes it difficult to distinguish the Toroweap Formation from the underlying Coconino sandstone. The

Cathedral Rock at Red Rock Crossing, perhaps Sedona's best-known landmark, is as geologically significant as it is beautiful.

sandy desert where Coconino sandstone originated was affected by the sea twice during the Late Permian Epoch. The sea, advancing from the west during its first transgression, covered the Grand Canyon to a considerable depth. These ocean waters produced the Toroweap Formation limestone in the Grand Canyon. Since the Sedona region was elevated somewhat during this period, it was only encroached upon by the sea, producing a sandstone formed in a near-shore, sandy environment.

A second advance by the sea occurred in the Early Permian Epoch, inundating northern Arizona. At this time, Sedona and Oak Creek Canyon were deeply submerged, and sediments of the Kaibab Formation were settling slowly on the ocean floor. Today, this formation yields a wide array of fossils. Corals, sponges, fishes, shellfishes, worms and crinoids are among the fossil forms that once thrived on a continental shelf. The erosion-resistant Kaibab Formation is the rim rock of the Grand Canyon and can be seen today beneath the lava caprock and "rim gravels" along Oak Creek Canyon.

The Cenozoic Era, which spans the past 64 million years of geologic history, was a period of great change for the Colorado Plateau. A regionwide uplift of the plateau occurred during the Laramide Orogeny, a 30-million-year period of mountain-building in western United States. This period spanned the latest Mesozoic Era and extended into the early Cenozoic Era. During this time, the southern margin of the plateau was uplifted in excess of 15,000 feet and tilted gently to the north. In central Arizona, the region now called the Transition Zone was uplifted as part of the plateau as well. During the Laramide Orogeny and throughout much of the Tertiary Period, the Transition Zone contained the high peaks of the Mogollon Highlands.

The mountains of the Mogollon Highlands initially were a part of the southern Colorado Plateau, being connected by a continuous ramp of sedimentary rock tilting gently to the north. On the surface of this ramp, streams transported gravel and cobbles northward from the highest southern peaks. Today, these deposits of alluvium are found near the southern margin of the Colorado Plateau. Informally named "rim gravels," they are important evidence in the interpretation of the geologic history of the area. Though the ramp connecting the present plateau with high mountains to the south is gone, diagnostic rock types found among the rim gravels reveal their origin. These metamorphic and igneous rocks closely match the basement rocks found today in the Transition Zone and thought to be the roots of the eroded Mogollon Highland mountain range.

Between 36 and 24 million years ago, erosion adequately removed the relatively soft sedimentary rocks of the Paleozoic and Mesozoic ages from atop the resistant basement rocks of the Mogollon Highlands, effectively disconnecting the ramp and ending the transport of alluvium onto the plateau. Coupled with this breakdown of the ramp, erosion further produced an escarpment between the present Mogollon Rim and the high country to the south. This early Tertiary escarpment, which may have had 2,000 feet of relief, was the first stage in the long development of the southern edge of the Colorado Plateau that we recognize today.

Following this erosion, during the period spanning 24 to 12 million years, faulting along the base of the ancestral Mogollon escarpment further developed the relief of the area. These faults dropped the land to the south, accentuating the difference between the early Mogollon Rim escarpment and the area that became known as the Verde Valley.

Between 15 and 6.5 million years ago, many geologically significant events occurred in the southern margin of the Colorado Plateau. Initially, movement along the nearly vertical Oak Creek Fault displaced the suite of sedimentary rocks previously described. This displacement produced down-to-the-east offset and created a zone of crushed and weakened rocks that is being eroded by Oak Creek, carving a canyon into the margin of the Colorado Plateau. Following this faulting, erosion of the plateau surface atop the eastern rim of Oak Creek Canyon beveled this area to create a southerly slope. This localized erosion is likely the reason for the lowered eastern rim of Oak Creek Canyon, which can be observed from the Oak Creek Overlook at the head of the canyon, and for a 600-foot-deep canyon carved into sedimentary rocks in the eastern rim above Manzanita Campground.

Coinciding with these events were repeated eruptions of black, basaltic lava from numerous vents along the southern margin of the Colorado Plateau from approximately 15 to 6.5 million years ago. At least seven separate eruptive cycles can be distinguished from the lava filling of the channel above Manzanita Campground. These deposits of lava altered the course of streams on the plateau surface and created an erosion-resistant cap, effectively protecting much of the record preserved in sedimentary rock. Beginning about 8 million years ago, massive amounts of basaltic lava erupted from the plateau surface and poured into the Verde Valley. These deposits, often called the "ramp basalts," are utilized by Interstate 17 to ascend the margin of the Colorado Plateau.

The changing of the earth's surface is a never-ending process. The collosal events described here — the three-mile uplift of huge areas of the earth's crust, the erosion of many thousands of feet of rock, the eruption of enough lava to form a gentle ramp down the Colorado Plateau — are unique to the Sedona area, but other unimaginable geologic happenings can be observed occurring elsewhere on the earth. These natural phenomenons provide information about earth processes, not necessarily end products. The immensity of geologic time cannot be overstated. Often, it seems earth scientists are rather casual when referring to the millions or billions of years required for a geological event to occur, yet it is this vast time factor that is the key to understanding earth history.

Nowhere is that more evident than in spectacular Sedona and beautiful Oak Creek Canyon.

Published by
Sedona Publishing Company, 271 Van Deren Road, Sedona, AZ 86336

©1996 and 1994, 1993, 1992 by Sedona Publishing Company

Reproduction of material in whole or part
without permission is prohibited.

Technical information regarding the geologic formation
of the Sedona area originally was authored by Kenneth
Thiessen, B.S., M.S., and subsequently was edited, revised
and included with text by Hoyt Johnson.

Printed by
Land O' Sun Printers, Scottsdale, AZ